By the same author

War in Medieval Society
Borderland (1984)
Lightning Country (1987)
The King of Ashes (1989)
Clay (1989)
The Confirmation (1992)
Y Felan a Finnau (1992)
The City (1993)
Heroes (1996)
No Hiding Place (1996)
Abergavenny (1997)
The Wine Bird (1998)
Ice (2001)
At the Salt Hotel (2003)
Sea Lilies: Selected Poems 1984-2003 (2006)
The Green Buoy (2006)
Trouble in Heaven (2007)
Tales of the Shopocracy (2009)
West Jutland Suite/Vestjysk Suite (2009)
The Forest Under the Sea (2010)
Fire Drill: Notes on the Twenty-First Century (2010)
A Year of Flowers (2011)
The Roaring Boys (2012)
Footfalls in the Silence (2014)
Wind Playing with a Man's Hat (2016)
Departure Lounge (2018)
Sherpas (2018)
Sunglasses (2020)
Afterlives (2021)
A Report to Alpha Centauri (2021)
Tsunami Days (2023)
Dunes of Cwm Rheidol (2023)
Kaleidoscope (2024)
Ice (2nd edition) (2024)

In the Shadow of the Yew

John Barnie

Cinnamon Press
:: small miracles from distinctive voices ::

Published by Cinnamon Press
www.cinnamonpress.com

The right of John Barnie to be identified as author of this work has been asserted by him in accordance with the Copyright, Designs and Patent Act, 1988. © 2026, John Barnie

ISBN 978-1-78864-192-0

British Library Cataloguing in Publication Data. A CIP record for this book can be obtained from the British Library.

All rights reserved. No part of this publication may be reproduced, stored in a retrieval system, or transmitted in any form or by any means, electronic, mechanical, photocopying, recording or otherwise without the prior written permission of the publishers. This book may not be lent, hired out, resold or otherwise disposed of by way of trade in any form of binding or cover other than that in which it is published, without the prior consent of the publishers.

Cinnamon Press is represented by Inpress

In the EU, we are fully compliant with GPSR (General Product Safety Regulation). Our EU GPSR Authorised Representative, via Inpress Books, is LOGOS EUROPE, 9 rue Nicolas Poussin, 17000, LA ROCHELLE, France E-mail: Contact@logoseurope.eu

Designed and typeset in Bodoni by Cinnamon Press. Cover design by Adam Craig © Adam Craig

For Ian McDonald

I believe that the world would look on unconcerned if the whole of mankind wiped itself out. It would create others. They might be cleverer.

Béla Zombory-Moldován

In the Shadow of the Yew

I

I want to correct the Book of Genesis
when Eve plucked the apple
it was from the Tree of Pain not Good and Evil
and from it carpenters adzed the Cross

    the Madonna's blue robes have faded to grey
    washed too many times in humanity's suffering
    slapped on stones by the still-flowing river

who is this extra chair for? nobody is coming
the bunting has already been taken down

        there are between one
        hundred and four hundred
        billion stars in our galaxy
        and a trillion galaxies in
        the observable universe
        blue shift... red shift
        not even a scanning electron
        microscope could tell us

        who or what we are

have hope, have courage, we sail on a
raft of expectations while in the sea below,
amphorae lie like skittles from a game
played long ago among the ribs of a ship

I passed my childhood and youth on the banks of the Usk
watched dippers among stones bobbing in watery light
saw rotting sheep tangled in willows, swam among eels

    when age began to reap him
    it would have been good to have said a prayer
    in an old church where the eagle
    bears a Bible's weight on its back
    with a cruel hook to the beak

this is the age of pills and neuroses
except in places where the land is dust
and the ribs of cattle stick through the skin

    why not sit still
    watch a nuthatch at the feeder
    a cat at the mouse hole
    roses unfolding

we have had a cargo cult for years
go into any supermarket
among humming refrigerators
bright polished light
pop tunes no longer popular but familiar
floating above our heads
and aisles full of everything the Earth
has ever produced, but tell me
where and who is the god

if you speak one language
you go round and round and round
in a goldfish bowl no matter
how clear the water how
green the weeds, everything
in the world beyond, a blur

    about sixteen million died in
    World War One between forty and
    sixty-five million in World
    War Two, we cannot keep Death
    from peering in our windows

afterwards when the terror subsided
there were only women keening over the dead
wringing their hands, raising them to the sky
mud mud and there they lay the loved ones,
also many they did not know but grieved over,
across the great plain for many days and weeks
only the bird of sorrow could be heard, black
and ugly it has to be said, easily mistaken
for a vulture that lands and tears out the heart

if they could, all creatures would look ahead
to the wilding of the Earth when cities
become the greatest trash cans ever known
and peregrines roost in their towers, humans
would shudder at the silence, at the lack
of momentum, the push of crowds, noise
for we are a noisy species filled with hate
and ambition and occasionally with love

I have a dream of entering a country church
it could be Llanwenarth, Kilpeck, Partrishow
the wrought iron latch lifted with a snap
opening the creaking door, removing my cap
the light will be grey while the sun shines outside
only here, I am inclined to believe, can anyone
hear humanity's cry, and our sorrow
at the echo's response, 'you are alone'

      are you coming to the Tay May Club
      we're going to have a good time
      we're going to tear it up bed slats and all
      we're going to stomp it on down to the bricks
      say little girl you with the red dress on
      landlady bring us some more liquor
      shoot out the lights, here come the police

the New Puritans
don't wear funny hats
or black clothes, but
wag their finger for a
ticking off, 'there's
one way; you can't walk
up and down here'

Waldsterben, that is a word for the human forest
our yellowing leaves through which
sparkle fingers of the Sun; autumn will turn to winter
pine forest ants will hunker down, the last voice
to be heard by our species, that of the mighty crow

they ate from a wooden bowl
gouged out of the table, slept
in wooden alcoves with stiff curtains
loaded hay in wooden lofts
herded cattle into wooden byres
bowed their heads at the low
wooden door, drew water at
the well in wooden buckets, hard
hard was the way, yet glancing
out of the small window they were
at least assured all of it was real

    'nobody is above the law' but who makes the law
    you see Truth and Justice wobbly at the knees
    as the statue of the latest dictator is raised
    by cranes, swayed gently toward its granite plinth

life should be grasped like the tail of a kite dipping and soaring
a fluttering, tensile hallelujah thing
if anything can give praise and shout for joy
it is a blue kite swooping at the end of a string

        I see him with a plastic bag tied over his head
        slumped sideways in the chair, a Hollywood horror film,
        third attempt, tri chynnig i Gymro, he might have said

autumn light slants across humanity
picking out its elongated shadow

we're going to terraform Mars
there's a breakthrough in the Elixir of Life
say the billionaires, terrible that
they too float on the tide of the universe
toward a shoreline of bones

        after a long life you'd think
        there was something to say, advice
        to give, but no, the young still bounce

tri chynnig i Gymro—three tries for a Welshman.

    on the trampoline, dogs bark,
    babies are cuddled, washing and ironing
    to do every week, the clock
    ticking on the mantlepiece as it
    always has done, to be human
    is to be mundane and to die
    almost by surprise

what harm I did to my mother and father
what harm they did to me
without intending, kindly people
backbone people you might say
of our little town society

    is it time to enter St Mary's again
    this time more humbly
    to admit, though the Church is wrong,
    it hears the cry of humanity
    and, though it cannot heal our wound,
    is the only field hospital left

these are dark steps polished by many feet

    the universe is light the universe is darkness
    meteorites and planetoids collide in emptiness
    here we are like hedgehogs, what can we say

II

Ignorance wanders across a desert
clothes flapping in a searing wind
snagging on thorns of the wait-a-bit tree

    they were picking the old lady up
    leaning over her concerned
    a branch brought down in life's storm

extremophiles have no thoughts
no sex, are unaware of death
guzzling sulphur from a fumarole,
we say consciousness is best
but how do we know?

    'this will do to be going on with'
    and he took the wad of notes
    from his dying father's wallet
    where it lay on the bedside table

if you could find peace and make amends
might it not be in this wood
beside quietly flowing Afon Peithyll
sunlight striking the canopy, koala-ivy
hugging the straight upstanding boles

    the radius of the universe
    is forty-six point five billion
    light years; that's some way to go;
    no good packing a suitcase
    trundling it on wheels; you'll
    never get from where you are
    to the unmanned border
    declaring yourself to yourself

        if the true state of the universe is unknowing
        a material finality should we not stop eating
        consciousness no more than a rip in the fabric
        a shaft of light out of a cloud fingering the sea

Cain, Cain his mother cried
she had lost both her babies
from one swift savage blow

      as to poetry it is like writing in a ditch
      while the tanks rush past, aerials swaying
      goggled commanders, slim barrels of guns
      steel tracks squeaking across ripped tarmac
      the poets lucky they are beneath notice
      with autumn's withered grass and flowers

science provided the crampons we used to climb into space
but we fumbled at the Pillars of Creation in the Eagle Nebula
six thousand five hundred light years from Earth

      in REM sleep the torturer's lids flutter
      as if the eyeballs want to escape
      but can't from what they have seen

six hundred million birds
have disappeared from Europe
what tonnage is that
how many hearts pattering faster
than rain on a canopy of leaves

      Jeremy Bentham said poverty
      is the unchangeable lot of our species
      look through the windows of your screens
      and tell me is it true

he thought of the past as a statue park
each statue someone he had known
and hurt; fir trees dripped condensation
on marble eyes, the park surrounded
by barbed-wire fences, over the Tannoy
a bass voice droning, 'I did it my way'

III

Everyone agrees he was a military genius
there was a bust of him in many a study
what are the deaths of a million men

few butterflies this year, no moths,
autumn turning on its side
for a winter of rough sleeping

> as a child I used to marvel
> at the parting of the Red Sea
> all those tiny figures scurrying
> quick! quick! over wet sand
> between quivering opalescent
> walls of glass-clear water

Les Murray, Sorley MacLean, RS Thomas
shooting stars across the night's
brilliant furnace, trailing poems

the coercive state
has handcuffs on its coat of arms
prison bars, an ear and an eye
don't be one of those who
disappear in the forest
to the scraping of spades

> you think nature is tamed
> but it seeds itself in cracks
> pushes up through tarmac
> ready for the final assault

our brains are too large for our cockleshell bodies
producing *The Radetzky March* and the torturer's chamber
ethnic cleansing and the Sisters of Mercy

there are the salt flats and across them a figure
in fluttering robes who though you cannot see his eyes
has seen you and strides to you over the blistering territory

if there were a parting of the waves
specially for us, a one-time dispensation
to cross into the Promised Land...

IV

At a reading in Lampeter RS asked any requests?
a foolish thing to do 'A Peasant' 'No'
yet when paid for poems we published
always that plain postcard the following day
diolch yn fawr am y siec, dymuniadau gorau
few poets did that, and as to 'A Peasant' how many times
was Yeats asked for 'The Lake Isle of Innisfree'
the price of stamps on the cards rose year by year

once RS read 'The White Tiger' to academics
who twisted it and turned it in the light
who teased out every living thread of it
'bloody good poem though' said Les Murray
a guest from Australia that evening
who didn't sit in a chair but occupied it
in capacious seaman's sweater and woolly cap

it's hard to think of poets
walking around as if they were ordinary
RS glimpsed in Pwllheli from a car, an Aldi
plastic bag in hand, wild hair

> I saw him at a reception, too,
> where he took a sip of wine as if *in absentia*
> the lips expressing the mind's distaste
> preferring a ledge above a restless sea
> listening to the water's deep lungs
> surging and falling away

Les lauded Mrs Thatcher
with a jovial Buddha smile,
invited to India 'fat men
are holy there'

they were not introduced
that evening when they circled round
the white tiger in its restless cage

diolch yn fawr am y siec, dymuniadau gorau—thank you for the cheque, best wishes.

V

Abel and Cain were pre-electric men
neither owned a computer
the horror they saw happened around them
Abel practising cruelty don't forget that
hitting his sheep along their spines
to harry them to the slaughter

    Derek has invited me round for a beer
    Derek is a perfectly decent ordinary man
    why do I think of swallows departing
    ospreys launching from their roosts
    to chance it across perilous seas

there is a jumping-off point into the dangerous unknown
a fighter pilot has it which is why he carries a pistol
to shoot himself in the mouth if he crashes with ant-people
he dropped bombs on moments before running to the wreckage

    seven-o-five-a.m. the old question rises again
    how many good poems are there in a generation,
    like finding diamonds in the sand at Ynys Las,
    here? no that is a piece of bottle glass, here?
    bottle glass again; Sorley MacLean found them
    on his misty island, in sands too in the Desert War
    a keening in that modest man whose sonorous
    words grew out of Skye's heather and whin

abandoned spiders' webs
hammocks for dust in the shed
spiders move on like the one
outside the window now
spinning its tensile trap for
luckless flies, cruel? no
the universe too is a web
stars and galaxies its flies

I've seen the tourist pictures
the screen savers of mountains
forests, deserts, multi-coloured
birds, lions, alpacas, pristine
worlds which humanity might
have just discovered bursting
in from what they destroyed

VI

As Conrad's pilot entered the snug
all girth, rain glistening off waterproofs
what I remember are his drinker's red veins
in cheeks and nose, a rough night to be at sea
Hokusai weather he might have said

>   poor Heyst he tried to hold life away
>   brought up by that miserable father
>   what did it bring him except a frightened girl
>   and his own humanity leaning out
>   to protect her, but it couldn't be done
>   when she lay shot in his arms
>   and the bungalow burned to the ground

the Jewish merchant of Costaguana
feared life all his life until, strung up
by the hands tied behind his back
arms bursting from their sockets,
he spat in his torturer's face

was it honourable to ask to be shot
there in the Lithuanian forest
where he stumbled over his dead horse
where he wore rags over his rags
in a white land under a white sky
frostbite on his cheeks?
was it honourable?

>   Stanley must have met Kurtz
>   though there is no record
>   and it could have been coincidence
>   each ramming heads on poles, each
>   wanting to exterminate the brutes
>   by which they meant themselves

>   >   who would have thought a hand
>   >   could turn into a snake
>   >   its head inching from the curtain

>   with a vial of poison, the great
>   de Barral, the shaky financier
>   adrift on the gently rolling ship

Conrad was writing in the study on a warm afternoon
French windows open, curtains breathing gently
only the scratch of his pen on sheets of paper
disturbing the peace until a shadow crossed the threshold
followed by one of Jessie's friends, her light
floral summer dress rustling as she tiptoed in
there you are, Mr Conrad, scribbling away again!

VII

Here he comes with the swagger
of a gangster, the little bullet-proof
eyes flicking from side to side
as he strides through golden rooms
through doors so high they dwarf him
'Politkovskaya' someone murmurs
'don't tread on his shadow now'

    as to the rape of the Sabine women
    it goes on all the time; women beware
    men after the walls are breached
    after tanks appear in the suburbs

in a perfectly ironed white shirt
he explains why we should vote for him
Justitia is blindfolded
she cannot see what is going on

let's say the species is criminally insane
do we really want it colonising Mars drilling on the Moon
making a desert out of deserts with a Galil Sniper

    my father was a soldier manqué
    running with a rifle through golden fields
    the little Abergavenny shopkeeper
    plucked from his town by 'events'

        London Warsaw Berlin Hamburg
        Dresden Leningrad Stalingrad
        Tokyo Nagasaki Hiroshima

VIII

Alexander paced the quarterdeck
when a gust of wind blew his crown
into the water; a sailor retrieved it
placing it on his head to swim back
the tyrant rewarded him with gold
then had him whipped for *lèse-majesté*
this was reasonable and not unfair

    dancing bears, boxing kangaroos
    caged tigers, the organ grinder's
    monkey, dogs leaping through
    hoops of flame, everything done
    to claw animals down to our level

suddenly it all seems meaningless
ice cream in the sun on a garden table
that can never be reconstituted
bad acting in a mediocre play
with a sprinkling of an audience
who throw their programmes away
when they exit onto the street

    we played at the Zanzibar last night
    there was a good crowd, in times like these
    people want fun, we are the fun loving species
    even in the ruins children play pitapat
    a draughtsboard is balanced on concrete rubble

Francis Bacon never painted 'The Screaming Judge'
the Nazis got there first at the People's Court
it would have been a study in grey of a little man
whose terrible power made him feel big who
thought he looked down from a great height
casting judgement and humanity into the flames

they must have painted by the light of tallow lamps deep in the caves
then one sweep round with the glimmering yellow to admire
before stumbling out into the Sun and air or perhaps it was night
so absorbed they had forgotten time, clasping each other's shoulders

IX

Prowl around the little church on a winter's evening,
whippy twigs of elms lashing the sky; the Grendel of our times
eaten by envy that there in the dim light shining through stained glass
the congregation of the timid and the old have something
he can never have, hope and prayer on the deck
of the Earth's ship as it wallows deeper in the storm

>that's what they were doing
>as the jets flew overhead,
>urinating up against a wall
>do you believe in life, one asked
>the other shrugged his shoulders
>as the bombs began to fall

you see how violence intrudes its quartz into the rock of our existence
small men driving big tanks churning mud as they manoeuvre into place

>and then there are the boxers
>the raw boned; women at the ringside
>in stiletto heels yelling for the spattering
>of blood and saliva, for bruised faces,
>dogs in remote barns put to savage
>one another as men place their bets

Autumn turns craftily away from Summer
swallows have got news of it, cold winds sweep leaves
the year's accountants are balancing the books
Winter's skirmishers have appeared in the hills

seen from here the stars are malevolent eyes
who hate to see life's challenge to inanimate matter
Venus Mars Jupiter Pluto, on to planets unnamed,
galaxies to which we have appointed numbers
what right had we to leave footprints on the Moon
that will last for millions of years after the death of life

X

Wordsworth talked too much about himself, RS
had that Easter Island look, yet I took their poems
on city buses where men hawked and spat
on top deck floors, ceilings hugged by
cigarette smoke seeking other men's lungs

    how could I know that leaving
    the hills and rivers where I grew up
    was a stab in the back betraying
    no one other than myself, never
    again could I make myself right

        poems can have meanings
        beyond what they say which
        sometimes hardly matters

the problem with the English is their dreams
of heraldic lions and *Dieu et mon droit*
in lands where everyone calls them Bwana

    the Welsh played their parts too
    the Prince's playthings little
    cockatoos who could speak a few words
    if you fed them bread and dripping

'in the land without a people the people without a land
blew up our homes, used rubble to pave roads
we fled across, keys in our pockets'

        I've been thinking about what good thought is
        pulsing in the brain like watching green blips
        travel across a hospital monitor, eventually
        it will be announced that thought is dead
        throughout the expanding burning universe

XI

What do you make of the jot and tittle of being here
I was in Operations when word came down
two hundred and seventy millions killed in the first strike
you don't have to be a brainiac to know we had won

    ferns spread their spores everywhere
    on Krakatoa they were the first
    they will be the last when crows and rats
    have given up, cockroaches conceded

the Doomsday Clock says nineteen seconds to go
no prospect of a leisurely breakfast
Jesus floats away like a bubble of air

BUT
I want to tell you how in winter
snow crept up to the black lips of Nant Iago
running with intensified crystal clarity
how twisted broken stems of bracken
pierced snow blanketing the Rholben
how the mountain oaks stood solid
furred with moss and snow, not a bird
to interrupt the silence, punctuated
by the Nant, except for a distant raven

    then you are walking at the foot of the Sugar Loaf
    gleaming white to the dew pond on the Deri
    that frozen little eye that hard little eye
    you can run and slide across with frosted breath
    getting there your feet will rise on a crusted
    glittering surface that collapses under your weight
    up-down up-and-down until your cheeks are red
    and you unbutton your coat, loosen your scarf

don't you think this is something the eagle
would tell the child

and all the while the valley below
misted in grey; hoar frost on the fields
chimney smoke hovering over streets
the town-hall tower's copper green
the one outstanding colourful detail
and you alive on the roof of the world

XII

Amerika is spending one point five
trillion on upgrading its nuclear
deterrence we are the rabbits chewing
on lettuce pushed through the netting
whatever we do we must believe we
are free, as Amerikans believe they are
good, let us apply greasepaint tears

    commercial travellers at my father's shop
    wore shabby-smart, brushing suits and trilbies
    in Commercial Hotels, displaying 'new lines'
    that were sure to sell, ready with order books;
    who were they? we have no names, lost
    like the Cybi canalised beneath the town;
    Blaenafon next, Brynmawr, then Nant-y-Glo

my ability to read poetry
precedes me to the grave
I wonder what these starbursts
mean as I turn a page

    isn't it clear
    poems are footprints
    of the human mind

where is technology taking us? nobody knows
we are leaving the orbit of humanity
headed into deep space with no reachable planet

at the edge of the forest animals are uneasy
humans have been seen trees falling monkeys screaming
hummingbirds, anteaters, vanishing in flames

XIII

**There is no redemption
because there is no God**

So there he was in St Mary's Church again
where the de Bohuns tried hard to pray in alabaster tombs
beneath armoured effigies, their secret being
for centuries they had been reduced to dust

when age placed rough sacking around his shoulders
he looked back on a miniature town beside a model railway
little people waiting for the train, woolly smoke rising from chimneys
a stationary milk float in an empty street, trees with flossy canopies

    a poem seems healthy until it takes sick
    dies and is buried in an unmarked grave

his mother in the tiny kitchen's
steam and clatter of saucepans
cooking grace meals every day
for the family to sit around
exchanging pages of the *Daily Mail*

    war war looking up
    into Pathé Newsreels
    projected by a beam
    of smoky light across
    the Pavilion's void

once I thought I glimpsed a stork
white against a ploughed brown field
the car was speeding toward our destination
no time to spare for contemplation
of a different way of being

    shards of bone, blood-stained cloth
    pieces laid out on a laboratory table
    a challenge to the forensic scientist
    convinced there was coherence once
    a friend, a colleague, a lover, even

XIV

Enthusiasm is as easy in Europe
as disillusions are in Africa
at the first step the dreamed of light
is changed into darkness
and every unexpected obstruction
signifies disaster

the natives became troublesome so after camping in a village
Stanley sent two parties of men to punish them
they shot two natives and brought back quantities of chicken and food
from the villages around; they brought the head of one of the natives
and stuck it on a pole close to our camp as a warning

> the more experience and insight I obtain into human nature
> the more convinced do I become
> that the greater portion of a man is animal

when I killed the crested crane its mate flew up
uttering the most pitiful cries
it even followed the man at a distance
who was carrying the body of its dead companion
one felt like a murderer

> Dr Schweinfurth will be greatly surprised
> at the discovery of a citron fruit

drums had just beat to knock off work in the station
he opened his eyes and stared at me clutching my hands
saying *Ward, Ward! they're coming! listen!*
yes they're coming, now let's stand together!
he was thinking of the old times when drums signified war;
as I supported him to administer brandy with a spoon
he drew a long breath and his pulse stopped

this morning I cut off the heads of two men
and placed them on poles
one at each exit from the bush into the plantation

the fact is that humanity, be it white or black
becomes mightily changed by the absence
of such civilising influences as a good dinner

as four o'clock sounded from Big Ben Stanley opened his eyes
and said *what is that?* I told him it was four o'clock striking
four o'clock he repeated slowly *how strange! so that is Time! strange!*

the men say a number of women
came down to the river's edge
and turning their back on them
slapped a certain part in derision
they were quite naked

This section consists of quotations, slightly altered, from the journals and memoirs of Gaetano Casati, Joseph A. Moloney, A.J. Mounteney Jephson, Emin Pasha, William Stairs, Dorothy Stanley, H.M. Stanley, and Herbert Ward.

XV

One evening as the Sun went down over the savannah
an upright ape looked at itself in a rare pool in this dried-up land
and saw that it was good, so began the inversion
because God did not create Man in His image
Man created God in his and has lived with it ever since
praying to a reflection in that long-forgotten pool

we see ourselves too in the Fall
expelling ourselves from the garden
when the serpent whispered
you are lords of it all

    that's why the universe is alarming,
    where to locate God in interstellar space
    is he to be found in dark matter
    present yet invisible? theologians
    crack knuckles, hunker under the Cross

and what about caretakers, humanity in disguise
wielding twig brooms to keep Earth green
motorways do not shift on their foundations
when news is broadcast that a flower has been saved

if you climb into religion's attic
you'll find dusty boxes of bones
painted marionettes with slack strings
instruments of torture, pilgrims' tokens
a postcard from Ynys Enlli where
twenty thousand saints are buried

    he always wore black shoes and a suit
    as if no funeral could take him by surprise
    what he wore for his own I never asked
    never saw into the vestibule of his coffin

on the other hand Bastet
goddess cat of the Egyptians
with a gold ring in her right ear
I could fall for that

XVI

A missile collapsed the last tenement
who then counted the dead? the grey men of Hades?
they had gone home to loving wives, celebratory dinners
who counts the crows and rabbits shot in the fields
may there be another war to finish the job

grey-and-white film for grey-and-white lives
a surprise then to learn they died in colour

    the question is simple
    who is to be
    as General Hamley said
    masters of the smoking ruins

        yet and still yet and still
        there was a farm near Abergavenny
        where the farmer's wife placed apple pies
        hot from the oven onto the table
        there were eggs in the henhouse
        warm to the touch

there's nothing like bombing
to make everywhere look like everywhere else
Warsaw Khan Yunis Beirut Cologne
dust and wreckage, people stumbling
with baggage which is mostly
a broken version of themselves

the greatest freedom is when you release the bomb
and bank to the right climbing steeply into absolute blue
at which moment it is as if your feet are planted on air
and there is no Earth as you rise and rise toward the Sun

XVII

Asked if H-bombs were safe in their silos
he said of course and never to be used
peace guaranteed by preparedness
for annihilation

> outside a song thrush sang
> primrose yellow its breast
> streaked with brown

>> this unique wandering ape
>> landing on the Moon
>> eyeing the deserts of Mars
>> how can it not trash itself?

we'reheretobringyoufreedomnfuckinDEMOCRACY
shouted across rolls of razor wire
separating his anger from that of the crowd

>>> I don't know who I am
>>> in the past I knew
>>> but now I am unsure,
>>> my mother never was so,
>>> rocking her desire
>>> in her arms

the Usk flows past the town as it always has done
the grey Usk, the blue Usk, the brown Usk stronger
than a strong man's arm ripping trees from their sockets
slamming them into old stone bridges from Brecon
to Llanellen; after the next war the Usk will flow on,
likely carrying the dead with the rest of its detritus

> 'all action is bound to be harmful, it is devilish,
> that is why this world is evil upon the whole'
> so Axel Heyst

XVIII

Why she gassed herself, why he hanged himself
we do not know, though Conrad may be right
self-destruction 'is not an act of savage energy
but the final symptom of complete collapse'

    not even summer could detain them
    swifts screaming round golden cupolas
    cloisonné butterflies sipping
    from the bluish cones of buddleia

        the Moon rose doleful as ever
        working things out it could be said
        amid the dust of the regolith

don't get me wrong 'life is forced upon us
whether we will or not, we do not agree to accept it
therefore we are quite justified in ending it'
Mounteney Jephson thinking against his age

    what keeps the old in rocking chairs
    looking out from stoups across fields of time
    'that's where the great flood of 'Twenty-eight
    came bearing down, many were drowned'

then there was Radomir and his men
making their way across high ranges to Italy
eating grass, the taste of utter defeat

        the past raises its head wave after wave
        before flopping on sand or beating itself
        against lofty hard implacable cliffs

my cousin had it right *'battle on'*
a fighting retreat blemished by age
that pinned its medals to his flesh,
in a boxer's crouch at ninety-three
'come and get it', meaning his life

XIX

They baptised her Melody 'a nice name for a girl'
but now she is old, the piano tuner gone,
if she tinkles a few notes discords abound
the piano cannot stretch to music, far better
close the lid, walk toward what's left of the day

    small Australopithecines looking up at the velvet night
    punctuated by so much radiance, could they have been the first
    to hear the distant melancholy 'Musick of the Spheres'

humanity is running on empty it cannot be helped
the hope is technology will lead us by the hand
for one more trip to the supermarket
one more holiday abroad;
tap the dial to no end, the needle hovers on red

    gorillas pause in their feeding
    sheep look up from the fields
    there goes a flock of cockatoos

when he died she let the garden go
a surprise how vigorous nature can be
the greenhouse overwhelmed, the lawn
a knee-high tangle of grass, deer
wandering in from the fields to nibble
while she cradled her grief

explorers marched in silence through the Ituri
the only sound they said was the whoosh and crash
of some giant giving up in the distance collapsing
with a smash of branches and leaves conceding
the dance to immense clouds of yellow butterflies

    there's a party on the cruise ship
    everyone's dining at the Captain's table
    afterwards a dance, flags of the nations
    bunting, streamers, the ship lit up

sailing to the Paradise Islands
welcomed by garlands, hula dancers
as if Gaugin had never died
or time moved on crab-wise
toward the fathomless dark ocean

XX

Screen savers prepare us for the day,
castles above winding rivers, villages
with red roofs where you can imagine
exotic food and wines friendly locals
described in postcards home, the past
grown over by the exuberance of life
only revealed when a skull is ploughed
to the surface with its universal grin
of a man or woman shot against a wall

nobody knew what the Bodger's game was or even if he had one, nobody knew his real name either. Dwarfy said he knew but Dwarfy couldn't tell you the time without lying. Anyway this Saturday we were in the Lucarno playing snooker, 'Men Only' because this was before PC and Women's Lib, and Dwarfy had his head down about to give the reds a good smack, that withered arm of his executing a quick jab to the end of the cue, when *bang-crash* the doors burst open and in stumbled Bodger, blood streaming down his face like the Mekong Delta, and behind him the police who tackled him to the ground saying 'got you, you bastard' and the rest, well you know the rest, it was all over *The Chronicle*...

'the cemetery of hopes' (Conrad)
I wonder where that is now
hidden perhaps like Angkor Wat
in the jungle we call the mind

> I've often thought of that wasp
> laying its eggs in a caterpillar
> to be eaten from the inside out
> what better definition of horror
> do you want, yet all impersonal
> no animus, no horror therefore
> the economic imperative leading
> to Earth's unpalatable truth

so it must be for the torturer the true one that is
whose job is quite impersonal like a swimming pool at dawn
water rippling in a breeze indifferent as to whether
bathers come or not; 'to intrude pleasure into torture
is to become a monster, not master of the task at all'
that's the professional view elicited from the wasp

XXI

Dear Brothers and Sisters when the Dove came down from the Ruined Tree it brought Spectacular News even to the Muslim Mother cowering with her Child as American bombs blew up their lives *Jesus Saves!* what does it matter if you lose a hand or a foot what does it matter if drones hover above you, they say Jesus was a Jew but He was made in America and if He came again He would wear *Stars-and-Stripes* on His battle jacket, surely you know this, surely you know that when a rosy red dawn fills the eastern sky and our jets take off to bomb evil, Jesus is with them, and that if you are saved how great the joy to the clashing of cymbals in the military band; one just man in Fallujah and we would have spared you all, even now among the ruins listening for a child's cry, you can receive His blessing *HALLELUJAH! HALLELUJAH! AMEN! AMEN!*

    I've heard them practising over the hills
    Americans or British it's hard to say
    decent chaps or automatons swapping one state
    for the other after a good breakfast

        you rarely see them above the clouds
        just the black roar of their engines
        as if they circle looking for something
        to relieve the burden of what they are

'after the unhappiness of being born
I know of none greater than that of
giving life to a man' (Chateaubriand)
discuss

Jesus cursed the barren fig tree whipped the money changers
went off in a pwd into the desert; Joseph and Mary despaired;
the word Schadenfreude had not been invented yet
so villagers took a knowing stroll past the parents' house

pwd—sulk.

when he'd read *The Oxford History of Ancient Egypt* to the end
the colonel put it down, *'straordinary*, he said

> *if you're dead long enough*
> *someone will come*
> *and dig you up*

XXII

There's a new kind of *Special Delivery*
a missile so fast you don't hear it
as you raise a cup of tea to your lips
or sit on the steps of the air raid shelter
to enjoy the warmth of the Sun

> the man with pincer eyes sent it
> whose priests swing incense
> blessing technology

Mentuhoteb deified himself in his House of Millions of Years
not bad going making Hitler seem modest with a Thousand Year
Reich not asking much his head on stamps the right to kill whomever
he pleased swastikas' iron throwing devices to hurl at sub-humans
but all reduced in the end to mummified ambition, ruins, loss

> if we wiped ourselves out
> who in the universe would know

should we think like this, shouldn't we hurry with Mary and Joseph,
to be in that cattle shed for the birthing, with the blood-warmth of
beasts, the bright star shining, the Wise Men opening their packs and
offering gifts, a transformatory moment on that little spot of Earth; I
felt this at the school Christmas carol service, cold hills all around
and snow winnowing out of the darkness; we were a cup held in the
hands of the town as we sang with the crystal voices of children

it was a dark night
rain beat upon the hospital window panes
the old lady raised herself in the bed
'does anyone here hold anything against me?'
no, mother, no! whispered her daughter
the old lady sank back on the pillows
and never spoke again

> we are all marginalia
> the question is
> what is the book

XXIII

Here I want to record Mrs Rowlands, North Street,
one of the town's marginalia for sure
her goitre a lifebelt holding her head above water
her loneliness reflected in the mirrors

death is one of the more resilient commodities, what is it
trading at today 'I have a Glock for personal use' said the would-be
president of the United States 'and if anyone breaks into my home
I'll blow them away'

    but then there are babies, little masterful buddhas
    sitting up in prams with unfocussed eyes
    splashing with their hands if happy
    they have no future because the future does not exist
    also no past with its vanishing point
    in row after row of military graves

        people crowded round the Well of Happiness
        no water here no water somebody cried
        and they shouldered their bundles and packs
        headed for the stark brown Black Mountains
        the barren rockiness of St Mary's Vale
        following the trail of what had been Nant Iago;
        water, they found, was all they wanted
        as they crossed the parchment of the Rholben
        reading the hieroglyphs of its withered oaks

my ghosts mean nothing to you
and your ghosts mean nothing to me
though we meet in open boats
adrift on the greasy swell of the sea

      being ordinary
      and not a fiery wasp
      that's a good thing
      is it not

XXIV

What do we do now what do we do now what do we do now
what do we do now what do we do now what do we do now
what do we do now what do we do now what do we do now
what do we do now what do we do now what do we do now
what do we do now what do we do now what do we do now
what do we do now what do we do now what do we do now
what do we do now what do we do now what do we do now
what do we do now what do we do now what do we do now
what do we do now what do we do now what do we do now
what do we do now what do we do now what do we do now
what do we do now what do we do now what do we do now
what do we do now what do we do now, what do we do now
what do we do now what do we do now what do we do now
what do we do now what do we do now what do we do now
what do we do now what do we do now what do we do now
what do we do now what do we do now what do we do now
what do we do now what do we do now what do we do now
what do we do now what do we do now what do we do now
what do we do now what do we do now what do we do now
what do we do now what do we do now what do we do now
what do we do now what do we do now what do we do now
what do we do now what do we do now what do we do now
what do we do now what do we do now what do we do now
what do we do now what do we do now what do we do now
what do we do now what do we do now what do we do now
what do we do now what do we do now what do we do now
what do we do now what do we do now what do we do now
what do we do now what do we do now what do we do now
what do we do now what do we do now what do we do now
what do we do now what do we do now what do we do now
what do we do now what do we do now what do we do now
what do we do now what do we do now what do we do now
what do we do now what do we do now what do we do now
what do we do now what do we do now what do we do now
what do we do now what do we do now what do we do now

XXV

There are one billion forty-seven million vehicles in the world
what do you make of that trundling across red mud tracks in Africa
six lane highways in New York

not enough not enough
in Antarctica only fifty
a sprinkling abandoned
on Mars and the Moon

𝕳𝖊𝖆𝖗𝖙𝖘 𝖔𝖋 𝕺𝖆𝖐 that's the English
hawking *Big Issues* on corners of streets
sitting on pavements with cardboard signs
'I am homeless and hungry please help'

POLITICIANS
you lie so much
when you tell the truth it seems a lie
the lie direct or the lie indirect
everything you say is a lie
because you say it

on a huge hill cragged and steep truth stands
and he that will reach her about must and about must go

> *what is truth said jesting Pilate*
> *and would not stay for an answer* oh truth!
> that is far too difficult a way to go

I had exercise books stuffed with facts, as then known,
though not so real as the Usk's rippling shallows
where mottled loach shouldered themselves among
stones furred and slippery with algae while sand martins
flitted, the tireless brown cave dwellers of the banks

---

on a huge hill, John Donne; *what is truth*, Francis Bacon, both modified.

XXVI

There is a crackling in the air an old lady puts her head out at the door raises her face to the black roil of clouds extends a hand for the first pattering of the downpour; on a far hill the three crosses appear again as they did before the last and she can just descry the three crucified men as tiny silhouettes; that time she cradled a baby when the tanks plunged past this time she has nothing in her arms as the old black cat rushes in out of what comes next

> she had a prolonged affair with cancer
> they danced all night when the hospital lights were low
> while the other patients slept uneasily in their beds

he had killed himself during the War
but vigil was kept from a house on the cliffs
by a lover who was faithful
long after the troopships came home

a red kite beating with strong wing strokes across a grey dawn

after the Bomb was dropped, the sky lit up with a hushed light over the Cambrian Mountains followed by a distant glass-rattling rumble, no one knew what it was except that it was something bad, even the sparrows stayed hushed in bushes and hedgerows; news came intermittently that London was gone; in Aberystwyth supermarkets were denuded, people hoarded what they could, very few cars travelled the streets; we were lucky, the weather-vanes of the hawthorns leaned west to east on the hills as they always had done, the prevailing wind taking fall-out across the North Sea; waiting was the worst, as if a silence had drifted throughout the land, people looking east where the future lay; it came in cars and trucks loaded with bedding, loaded with people with empty faces out of a world stripped of meaning

> a roseate tern on Knudshoved
> fluttering brilliantly its
> tail streamers like ribbons on a bride's
> bouquet to be caught in the air

a mountain bluebird in Saskatchewan
blue as the bluest lapis lazuli
in the washed-out after-winter land

goldfinches sprinkling themselves
across autumn fields on the way to town

a great spotted woodpecker at the feeder
ripping out seeds with its jackhammer

great crested grebes steaming in line on Esrum Sø
their wake a tailor's scissors cutting through silk

XXVII

The American empire is a big thing
it tells itself it has a big heart
and has a big military to keep it pumping
the British had an empire too
and some believe still in its heart
though cremation shrivelled it
on the sands of many shores

    there she goes walking toward the early morning flight
    love's failure glistening in her eyes
    the harsh grey landscape
    denying it could have been different

pat the past on its head and let it go to school
there is much it didn't know that you know now
and can tell it, if the past can listen still

    eighty-three
    and the bowman in the door
    'shoot straight
    then shoot no more'

what was he like? it's a long time ago but I remember his intensity; when you were talking with him he didn't so much look you in the eye as stare at you; I found it disconcerting, rude, even; he had a button-holing way of jabbing your chest with his forefinger when making a point, yet he had a limp handshake, something I dislike, suggesting lack of character or lack of interest, or both; you couldn't have a conversation with him, he was a monologuist with an urgent message to give you and you were supposed to listen; he had no sense of humour so you couldn't relax, have a joke in his presence; and you were with him or against him; he was remarkably well informed on religious law, delighting in tripping you up over abstruse detail; perhaps he was manic-depressive, it's difficult to say; he was never diagnosed, so far as I know; his mood could change with a snap of the fingers, and then watch out; but all that stuff wandering in the desert then coming back renewed, expecting you to drop what you were doing and follow him, just like that, it wasn't on; I never liked him, sad to say, and never trusted him, blowing hot and cold, with outbursts of anger and that irritating habit of always being right; so no, I didn't take to him at all

XXVIII

What is the poison in our heads lures us
toward trenches, howitzers, grenades, bombs
assassination the tyrant's ace
laid on the baize of human suffering

> undertakers are like sad crows
> they're not of course
> one keeps racing pigeons
> one likes a flutter
> another's proud of his daughter
> who's gone to college
> only in life's storms
> do they come flapping
> to crowd around our doors

one of the company of small-town gamblers I think it was Neil Pothecary explained to me that men who study form laying out a pound or two at the betting shop in Cross Street don't expect to get rich they expect to lose except when a treble comes up and money is passed beneath the metal grill by a bored indifferent woman; beautiful crumpled notes a jingle of silver, life worth living as they enter The Hen and Chicks the warmth, the low lights, subdued conversation, Tony reaching for a glass, pulling a pint before being asked

> *creulon* is a better word than 'cruel'
> it has the beak
> it has the claws
> it cannot be dislodged from its crag
> where it looks down
> on the human valley

'there was darkness before you were born
there will be darkness after you have lived,
in between, what then?'

fair point fair point
few can be said to follow light
many take the trodden path
many wade through marshes
among the stelae of dead trees
I myself have done less good than harm

XXIX

At her funeral the preacher said she was an unusual lady
then started playing Vera Lynn singing 'We'll meet again'
not bloody likely Geoff muttered as her coffin slid to the furnace

Governor Laffan's fern extinct Escarpment cycad extinct Heenan's
cycad extinct Blue cycad extinct Parlota cycad extinct Wood's cycad
extinct Yellow fatu extinct Superb cyanea extinct Galápagos
amaranth extinct Kalimantan mango extinct

>   my fingers are swollen at the knuckle
>   digits pointing in different directions
>   just like my mother always my mother
>   a haunting out of the dust in her urn

he arrived at the back door with a battered pickup housing a
grindstone and his five- or six-year-old son, did I have any knives to
sharpen, I didn't so I said no, I'm *desperate* he said, I could see this
was so and went to the kitchen returning with a knife which he
sharpened, I paid him, it was the end of the day, I never saw him
again

>   humanity is in its final phase
>   we have surrendered ourselves
>   spilled out our minds
>   into memory banks, say
>   we have friends we
>   have never met, the malign
>   prowl seeking to harm
>   truth is falsified
>   the computerised voice
>   says sorry says thank you
>   but does not mean it
>   says I love you
>   but cannot love

XXX

Sixteen and sentenced to death?
'there is no mercy
only the river of justice'

> surely Utagawa Hiroshige wanted to delight the world
> and did with A Hundred Famous Views of Edo
> is that not better than betraying light with tragedy

American prisoners wear orange jumpsuits
to humiliate them to deny they are one of us
in Russia it is otherwise where the Moscow heart attack
is fashionable again

Eastern hare wallaby extinct Desert rat kangaroo extinct Hispaniola monkey extinct Darwin's Galápagos mouse extinct Sardinian pika extinct Red gazelle extinct Japanese otter extinct Large sloth lemur extinct Desert bandicoot extinct

> 'RS Thomas *Poetry for Supper*' a maroon-red insignificant spine
> that had to be plucked out at Hudson's university bookshop;
> hungry for the Black Mountains and home I dined well that evening

> there used to be tree creepers in Bailey Park
> perhaps there still are leading vertical lives on bark
> unobserved by those walking through to town

in his day he was a ten pints a night man
the last time I saw him he was nearly blind
had given up drink was removing brambles
blocking an old garage door, bare hands
cut and bleeding seemingly without pain

> Francis Bacon understood the ferocity
> painting it as if angrily in a living blur
> of factory meat in a factory process
> a sprawl of tangled limbs afterwards

you can sense your innards
like an old coal-fired ship
every yaw in a storm threatening
a leak because you are rusty
because blockages may occur
because the warm raging heart
may burst, valves gone, life's
festival brought to an end

>   yet, yet
>   there may still be time
>   to paint miniatures of flowers
>   in a Chinese style
>   each brushstroke meticulous
>   and swift

XXXI

Are you thinking what I'm thinking
that great art is produced by wild dogs
pacing round the campfire which most of us
prefer to warm our hands by, turning backs
on the night forest where the dogs' eyes'
luminescence is an accusation and a threat

        not all of course, Eliot
        disguised himself as a furled
        umbrella, knelt at the Cross
        showering it with irreproachable
        tears as the poetry suffered

FORECAST
for the manufacturers of bombs it will be a good year
money passed in milliseconds from account to account
when the bombs start falling 'something must be done'
politicians announce raising inutile hands at the podium

Mysterious starling extinct Least vermillion flycatcher extinct North island piopio extinct Passenger pigeon extinct O'ahu 'akialoa extinct Laysan honeycreeper extinct Marianne white-eye extinct Dodo extinct Slender-billed curlew extinct

    there, caught at a glimpse
    from the corner of an eye
    a bird's silhouette's swift dash
    through a tangle of twigs
    against a grey winter dawn

        a mother told me that after her son died
        she would take his pullover from a drawer
        press it to her face for the fading odour
        of his life, all else having passed away

I once swam to a marker buoy in the sound between Sweden and Denmark, held on for a while then dived following the links of the chain one by one to their anchorage in the sand; that was a desolate place, the water a murky blur, the chain furred with algae, undersea life claiming it for its own

why are skulls always grinning
as if they'd enjoyed it hugely
and now could stare at the Sun

XXXII

Prince Philip took an interest in UFOs
rather odd for a 'bugger-off' sort of man
more prone to chasing hikers from his land
how had he construed spaceships hurtling
across light years of time vast desolations
buttering toast with a rasp of the knife

best not to have to make amends
the pilgrim stumbling at the door
where he'd hoped to be saved

>   who rolled the stone away
>   stole the body, left the grave cloths;
>   forensics examines the cave
>   with the dry light of reason

Tobias caddisfly extinct Kilosa noble grasshopper extinct Robert's stonefly extinct Mono Lake diving beetle extinct Spined dwarf mantis extinct Molokai damselfly extinct Togo red jewel extinct Ridley's stick insect extinct Kona giant looper moth extinct

>   I never met Hitler being four years old when he died
>   had I done so he would have patted my head
>   which was blond though my eyes were brown;
>   it is what dictators do, wearing the rictus of a smile

𝕿𝖍𝖔𝖚 𝕾𝖍𝖆𝖑𝖙 𝕹𝖔𝖙 𝕶𝖎𝖑𝖑 facing the war memorials
Jesus no longer in his cot or on the Cross
but rifle in hand leading the charge
if there were no gods it would be the same
there is no exchange for the currency of our species
unique and proud, unique and beaten down
children not suffered to come unto anybody
suffering instead amid ruins and flames

I met a fly on Aberaeron beach
with brown compound eyes
its abdomen a chequered board
for playing the game of life
what we were to each other
across tens of millions of years
I was unable to decide

XXXIII

There are a lot of turnings, a lot of overridings and underminings in a long life a lot of climbing spiral stairs in a deserted church where wood pigeons nest and flee with a clap of wings at your approach where with hands on the platform's battlements you look out across fields and woods, farms and villages, though not so far as cities, those forests of humanity, of anonymity, kinetic exuberance, rush of laughter, despair on park benches which the police dispose of

Victorian churchyards are best with alabaster doves perched on headstones quietly for a moment, the olive branch of peace in their beaks, or angels with alabaster wings folded in prayer or grief, almost female though not quite because these are heavenly beings, sorrow is transitory, and already many years ago they wafted the soul to invisible rejoicings, leaving us blind with hands outstretched, walking among yews that drop red poison berries in our path

Homo rudolfensis extinct Homo habilis extinct Homo ergaster extinct Homo erectus extinct Homo heidelbergensis extinct Homo neanderthalensis extinct Homo denisova extinct Homo floresiensis extinct

Homo sapiens

www.ingramcontent.com/pod-product-compliance
Ingram Content Group UK Ltd.
Pitfield, Milton Keynes, MK11 3LW, UK
UKHW041807090226
467841UK00002B/63